"[Jon's] wor‹
army wife, a
goose bumps

MW01268146

—Brooke Brown
(Army Wife)

"These are beautiful, inspiring & truthful pieces of poetry. They are some of the best I've ever read!!"

—Ontario Re'Shard,
funk and soul musician

"This is a very well written compilation of poetry that will tear at your heart strings. Grab your tissues as you sit down and enjoy this author's work."

—Sheila Reem,
member of the Patriot Guard Riders

"This is a very well put together piece. There is something in here for everyone, one can tell that a lot of thought and passion went into this. I highly recommend it, you won't be disappointed. I consider it an honor to have the privilege to put my loving stamp of recommendation on it, a beautiful piece of quality and verbal craftsmanship."

—Peter N. Peveto,
author of *Is It Me Can You Tell*

REFLECTIONS OF LIFE

A Collection of Poetry from a Soldier's Point of View

REFLECTIONS OF LIFE

JON M. NELSON

INTRODUCTION BY DUSTIN BOGUE

TATE PUBLISHING
AND ENTERPRISES, LLC

Published by Tate Publishing & Enterprises, LLC
127 E. Trade Center Terrace | Mustang, Oklahoma 73064 USA
1.888.361.9473 | www.tatepublishing.com

Tate Publishing is committed to excellence in the publishing industry. The company reflects the philosophy established by the founders, based on Psalm 68:11,
"The Lord gave the word and great was the company of those who published it."

Book design copyright © 2013 by Tate Publishing, LLC. All rights reserved.
Cover design by Joel Uber
Interior design by Jomar Ouano

Published in the United States of America

ISBN: 978-1-62510-332-1
1. Poetry / American / General
2. Poetry / General
13.02.18

Acknowledgment

There are a few people that I would like to recognize for helping me make this book possible. I'd like to thank my wife, Amanda, who is my muse and inspiration. She is the one that the entire chapter "Love of a Lifetime" is written for. There's also a special thanks to Dustin Bogue for his amazing heartfelt introduction. Thank you to all the others that have taken the time to endorse my book, your thoughts and opinions mean so much. I'd like to thank my parents, family, and everyone else who has supported and believed in me over the years. I'd also like to thank God for giving me the talent that I share with everyone with this book. There are so many other people that I would like to thank but I know I can't get to everyone. However, pretty much anyone who has had an influence in my life has impacted my thoughts in this book in some way.

Dedication

To all the men and women of the Armed Forces and to my daughter, Bailey, and the future generations that will succeed us in this world.

Contents

LOVE OF A LIFETIME

HUMAN NATURE

A DARKER SIDE

God's Beauty

Introduction

Ask any writer, they'll tell you: There's nothing like reading something or hearing something written from someone who has been there. The genuine article from a place that the rest of us can only imagine being. Immersed in the passages of *Reflections of Life*, I found over and over again the evidence of a man that has run, walked, crawled and curled up in a ball in these places. Since I was a very young child, I have often thought about what a feeling it must be to be a soldier, to protect and serve these United States of America. The pride, the fears, the longing for home, the brotherhood with fellow soldiers, the devastation of war... all there in my thoughts. It's all here in this book. It's real.

— Dustin Bogue,
country singer (half of the duo Brasher/Bogue)

AMERICAN PRIDE

As You Get Ready

You've grown up, and we're proud of who you've become,
You have chosen a career that can only be done by a few.
We ask that you don't forget just where you came from,
As you get ready to join and serve the red, white, and blue.

* * * * *

You have a difficult task and many challenges ahead,
But we know that you will face them head-on with pride.
When you leave home I hope none of your tears are shed,
As you get ready to go on this wild and adventurous ride.

* * * * *

The family is so proud that you're willing to fill the shoes,
Of so many others that have served in generations before.
You have too much fight in you to ever back down or lose,
As you get ready to make yourself into so much more.

* * * * *

We are ready to let you go and make it on your own,
So that you can serve and make this family so proud.
We look at you and see how much you have grown
As you get ready to stand out from the crowd.

Infantryman

I've been shot at, and I've been stabbed,
And I've been nearly burned alive.
Yet somehow through all of this,
I have managed to survive.

* * * * *

I have been tortured and left for dead,
And I've felt the excruciating pain.
After all the horror that I've seen,
It's amazing that I'm not insane.

* * * * *

I've had the enemy locked in my sight,
I had been trained to shoot to kill.
I could lay in the mud and rain for days,
Yet you wouldn't see me as I was still.

* * * * *

I always control the battlefield,
And I always lead the way.
I move stealthily to the target,
Whether it is at night or in the day.

* * * * *

I've lost my friends and comrades,
And yet I still have to carry on.
The battle is never really over,
Even for the ones that are gone.

Jon M. Nelson

* * * * *

I've held my buddy in my arms,
And slowly watched him die.
The sights I've seen are so bad,
That they have made me cry.

* * * * *

I've walked for many endless miles,
And never been able to rest.
I have received many battle scars,
And earned the medals on my chest.

* * * * *

After all the hell that I have seen,
Many times I thought I was a goner.
I am the first line of defense,
And I risk my life with honor.

Lay My Guns Down

* * * * *

As I gaze out upon the desert sky,
I sit and ponder and wonder why.
I left my life and family back home,
For this place where I search and roam.

* * * * *

What must I do in this desolate space,
Where I don't fit in, I'm out of place?
Every day I fight just to stay alive,
I must dig down for my internal drive.

* * * * *

As I'm trying to bring them peace,
I hope that the fighting will cease.
All I'm trying to do is lend a hand,
But I don't think they'll understand.

* * * * *

I'm always reminded that I don't belong,
Yet still I have to always remain strong.
With bullets and bombs that are all around,
Screaming is a deafening and chilling sound.

* * * * *

War is a hell no one should have to witness,
No one comes back without being a mess.
As I lay my guns down and return home again,
I'll always remember just where I have been.

Jon M. Nelson

Soldier Poet

* * * * *

On the battlefield he's always alert,
And not afraid to get down in the dirt.
Back home he will share his thoughts,
And talk about the nightmares he has caught.

* * * * *

He wears his uniform and serves with pride,
With his brothers and sisters by his side.
With a pen and paper he's able to express,
The horrors he's been through, he'll confess.

* * * * *

He proudly serves and has your back,
And is always ready for most any attack.
Yet he writes of peace and the world as one,
For hopes that the wars will soon be done.

* * * * *

He carries a weapon to defend himself,
Yet he won't pass up a cry for help.
He uses his words to bring the peace,
As he tries to put the world at ease.

* * * * *

He'll fight when needed and won't back down,
Amid all the chaos that is always around.
His words of wisdom seem to bring change,
And hopefully the peace can begin to exchange.

Freedom Isn't Free

* * * * *

Freedom isn't free, it's something we always hear.
As we listen to the voices echo loud and clear.
There are those that are willing to stand up for our rights.
They are the brave ones, who won't back down from any fights.

* * * * *

As they serve their families and their proud nation,
There's no telling when they'll see either one again.
Away from home, their family is each other,
They consider themselves as sisters and brothers.

* * * * *

So many times people will misunderstand,
But when you're sleeping, that's when they stand.
Everyone takes for granted who they really are,
They're defenders of freedom near and far.

* * * * *

When you think of your life, don't ever forsake.
Take time to reflect the sacrifices they make.
They give a sacrifice for the way that we live.
So salute a veteran, it's the least that you can give.

Aftershock

I never knew what obstacles,
May be lurking around the bend.
There had been many times,
I thought that my life would end.

* * * * *

I never knew who to trust,
I was in a world full of strangers.
Even though we were always alert,
It was hard to ignore the dangers.

* * * * *

Today there are still times when,
I wake up in the dead of night.
Even though I'm sound asleep,
I cannot shake that awful fright.

* * * * *

The memories always still haunt me,
I can't get them out of my head.
So often I look back and realize,
Many times I came close to being dead.

* * * * *

The war will never really be over,
For those who have lived through hell.
And as those thoughts always remain,
There are many stories we have to tell.

I Stand Ready

* * * * *

I've fought for my country,
And shed my blood for you.
I help keep this nation free,
And defend the red, white, and blue.

* * * * *

I stand ready to defend,
On this and foreign soil.
My duty will have no end,
For my country, I am loyal.

* * * * *

I stand to face my enemies,
If they decide to attack.
For you and your families,
I always have your back.

* * * * *

You can rest easy tonight,
Knowing that I am here.
I will stand ready to fight,
To help you calm your fear.

* * * * *

It is not always glorious,
There are times that I dread.
But I will stand victorious,
Until the moment I am dead.

Jon M. Nelson

Casualty of War

* * * * *

With a terrified look upon his face,
I wonder what he's doing in this place.
There are bombs exploding and bullets flying,
He's curled up in a corner, scared and crying.

* * * * *

I know that he did not ask to be here,
And I know he's overwhelmed with fear.
Where are the parents of this child lost,
As he screams out in this holocaust?

* * * * *

I can feel his pain as I see his tears,
But his cries will fall upon deaf ears.
The sounds of war drown him out,
As he continues to scream and shout.

* * * * *

I cannot grab him for he's out of reach,
I hear the incoming high-pitched screech.
The explosion threw me to the ground,
And he laid there lifeless without a sound.

* * * * *

Why wasn't I strong enough to save,
The boy too young to be put in a grave?
For this innocent casualty of war, I cried,
Because it was senseless that he died.

Red, Fight, and Blue

* * * * *

We're honored to be on this piece of ground,
Because we didn't get it by backing down.
There are things that are worth fighting for,
Even though nobody ever wants a war.

* * * * *

We always stand up for justice and liberty,
And ensure that we keep our nation free.
We stand up for those who are weak,
And we won't turn the other cheek.

* * * * *

We don't go out looking for trouble,
But we don't exactly live in a bubble.
This nation will stand against any attack,
And we are not afraid to retaliate back.

* * * * *

We always stand up for what is right,
Yet others still want to test our might.
We've proven ourselves in peace and war,
Someday we won't have to fight anymore.

Heart of a Soldier

* * * * *

As the sun burns down it bakes my skin,
I can feel my patience beginning to wear thin.
Walking endless miles in this scorching heat,
I can feel the sand burning my feet.

* * * * *

On my back I carry this unbearable load,
As I walk along this seemingly endless road.
The weight is so much that I can barely stand,
To get up off my knee, I need a helping hand.

* * * * *

It seems like we have been walking for days,
With hardly any sleep it all, it seems like a haze.
The exhaustion is beginning to take its toll,
I'll never get back all the time that they stole.

* * * * *

In every corner, I'm reminded of home,
Yet I have no choice but to continue to roam.
Oh, how I miss all the ones that I left behind,
And sometimes I wish I could just hit rewind.

* * * * *

Then I realize that they're the reason I'm here,
Even through all my pain and fear.
I had to come over here and leave them back,
So they wouldn't worry about another attack.

* * * * *

Even with the bullets and bombs trying to kill,
I have to move on by searching for my inner will.
I've seen many die and suffer before my eyes,
And I've faced my horrors as I heard their cries.

* * * * *

I do what I do for my friends and my family,
And to help keep this nation of ours free.
And for those who will criticize and condemn,
A soldier will even serve honorably for them.

* * * * *

Through all the pain and torture I will carry on,
For without me, our freedoms would be gone.
And whenever I feel I cannot go on anymore,
I always remember exactly what I'm fighting for.

* * * * *

I am one of the defenders of this great nation,
And I will always do my job without hesitation.
The heart of a soldier can never be broken,
As his actions speak over the soft voice spoken.

Old Glory

* * * * *

It waves over the nation so proud and true,
The majestic colors of red, white, and blue.
It's been through war, it's been through hell,
And still the colors have not fell.

* * * * *

A symbol of freedom, a symbol of glory,
If it could speak, one heck of a story.
It may be flown, and it may be hung,
Yet its song will always be sung.

* * * * *

Since the birth of our nation to the present day,
It's been symbolic of the American way.
Men have fought, and many have died,
To defend and protect this symbol of pride.

* * * * *

Some gave their all, but all gave some,
So this symbol could wave for generations to come.
Blood, sweat, and tears were shed for this flag,
So that on the ground it would never drag.

* * * * *

So salute with pride and show respect,
And proudly remember those who've died to protect.
Reminisce on this nation's proud history,
Every time you gaze upon Old Glory!

King James and Uncle Sam

* * * * *

I keep King James in a drawer by my bed,
And I say a prayer before resting my head.
I serve Uncle Sam proudly every day,
As I help protect the American way.

* * * * *

I try to hang on to every word,
As they preach what should be heard.
If they give the orders, I will follow,
Even if my pride I have to swallow.

* * * * *

I read the book to do what is right,
So I am able to head toward the light.
I do their work without question,
And I will serve without hesitation.

* * * * *

I'm always informed of what to do,
As they will always guide me through.
As they lead, I will proudly serve,
And I'll stand with a steady nerve.

* * * * *

As I march along in their footsteps,
I have come to learn to accept,
I'm going down the correct road,
Even as I carry this heavy load.

Jon M. Nelson

Walk A Mile

* * * * *

For centuries they have been in the fight,
Serving our country and doing what's right.
They have worked so hard to pay their dues,
I'm honored to walk a mile in their shoes.

* * * * *

They will answer the call when we need,
Filling their ranks is such a rare breed.
They won't give up or know how to lose,
I'm honored to walk a mile in their shoes.

* * * * *

They'll accomplish the mission despite fears,
And they fight through the pain and tears.
They may feel like quitting, but they refuse,
I'm honored to walk a mile in their shoes.

* * * * *

They helped keep this nation of ours strong,
And they fight injustice because it is wrong.
Yet you won't see this on the evening news,
I'm honored to walk a mile in their shoes.

* * * * *

There are so many that just cannot see,
What it takes to keep our country free.
This path, so few were proud to choose,
I'm honored to walk a mile in their shoes.

Now a Man

* * * * *

He can now proudly hold his head up high,
After doing things that would make most men cry.
Even after all the suffering and pain,
He knew it was worth it after what he gained.

* * * * *

The physical torture that he felt like he endured,
Was part of the process and thought he was cured.
All the long days and sleepless nights he suffered,
Had worked in the end because he now felt tougher.

* * * * *

Through dirt and mud he had to push himself along,
They were only obstacles that would help make him strong.
Some hand-to-hand combat was part of the fight,
That he knew would also help increase his might.

* * * * *

Learning to shoot, stab, and other ways to kill,
Went against his conscience and his inner will.
In the end he watched his mom cry tears of joy.
Standing there now was a man that left home a boy.

Last Ounce of Soul

* * * * *

They do their job without reward,
Which some would consider selfless.
They stand up for the weak,
The downtrodden, and the helpless.

* * * * *

A soldier's heart, mind, and soul,
Is to always do his best.
To stand up for the innocent,
The tortured and oppressed.

* * * * *

A soldier's life is difficult;
It always comes with a price.
Missed holidays and birthdays,
Are part of the sacrifice.

* * * * *

They may be away from home,
But their hearts are always here.
Halfway around the world,
Their loved ones hold them dear.

* * * * *

They do their best to guard freedom,
Against those that would do us harm.
They all come from the big cities,
Small towns and from the farms.

* * * * *

They come from different backgrounds,
But they share one single goal.
They will defend our nation,
With every last ounce of soul.

Folded Flag

* * * * *

It's given to a family when a soldier has died.
It's a symbol of their service with so much pride.
It is presented to them and followed by a salute,
And they'll jump when they hear the guns shoot.

* * * * *

It's a symbol for those who've answered the call,
And it's a reminder for those that may fall.
It is only presented for those who have served,
It is considered an honor that is well deserved.

* * * * *

The emotions are intense as the preacher speaks,
And the tears burn as they roll down the cheeks.
All of the soldiers will have their own story,
And theirs has ended as they hand over Old Glory.

* * * * *

Our freedom is earned by their burdened scars,
And it's a reminder as we look at the stars.
But remember that their life was never in vain,
Even as our hearts will feel all the pain.

* * * * *

As the star-spangled banner is folded tight,
It's a constant reminder of the soldier's might.
As we hold the folded flag, it's a way to remember,
The proud honor of our fallen service member.

A Soldier's Night Before Christmas

* * * * *

It was the night before Christmas, and all through the camp,
The soldiers had changed out of clothes that were damp.
Our weapons were slung and held at the ready,
Although it was Christmas, we still stood rock steady.

* * * * *

The soldiers were tired and laid in their racks,
It was a long day, and it was time to hit the sacks.
The chaplain had just given the evening prayer,
And it was time to doze off without a care.
When outside the tent something had exploded,
We all jumped up, and we locked and loaded.

* * * * *

Away to the door we had moved with haste,
Wondering what type of enemy we faced.
The moon shined so bright it gave us a clear sight,
Of what kind of horror we would face that night.

* * * * *

As we looked closer we saw out on the ground,
Exactly what it was that made that huge sound.
It wasn't a bomb that was dropped down from above,
It was a care package delivered with love.
The crate had broke open when it hit the sand,
Everyone gathered around to lend a helping hand.

* * * * *

There were cards and cookies and movies of all sorts,
We had sporting equipment for those who loved sports.
Now we had games to play, there were gifts for us all,
But as we looked, something made everyone stall.

* * * * *

The children outside of the fence were all crying,
And the way they looked, most of them were dying.
Without saying a word we all did decide,
To pass these gifts to the children freezing outside.
They knew not of Christmas or receiving toys,
So this was a first for these girls and boys.

* * * * *

As we handed them gifts and food for them to eat,
We knew they were thankful for giving them the treats.
As I watched them eat, I knew it wasn't enough,
So I started looking through some of my own stuff.
I found some candy and snacks not yet open,
And I could always get more of some notepads and pens.

* * * * *

It was not very much, but I gave what I could,
And the looks on their faces made me feel good.
The other soldiers soon followed my lead,
And this Christmas was one they'd remember indeed.

Reflections of Life   41

Military Wife

* * * * *

She's keeping the home fires burning,
While a dangerous living he is earning.
She has had so many sleepless nights,
While he's away fighting for our rights.

* * * * *

She's always ready to answer the phone,
When she hears his voice, she's not alone.
His months away just seems so long,
But she knows she has to remain strong.

* * * * *

She knew what she was getting into,
When she stood with him and said, "I do."
She realized she had to make sacrifices,
And have to stand steady during a crisis.

* * * * *

When she doesn't know the time length,
She has to search for her inner strength.
She always expects that knock at the door,
When they tell her he won't be home anymore.

* * * * *

No matter what, she'll always stand by his side,
Because her heart is filled with so much pride.
It may be difficult, but it is a chosen life,
As she stands in the ranks as a military wife.

Military Mom

* * * * *

I've watched you grow from a child,
Into the adult that you are today.
You used to be so reckless and wild,
And you have come such a long way.

* * * * *

Now you proudly defend our nation,
And help keep this country free.
And you do all this without hesitation,
I'm just as proud as I can be.

* * * * *

There are times that I worry to death,
But I know you're doing what you must.
You'll defend us to your last breath,
Because in you and God I trust.

* * * * *

When I heard you joined the military,
I won't deny that I had cried.
But looking back now I can see,
How you filled me with so much pride.

* * * * *

My eyes always well up with tears,
Whenever I see you in uniform.
But I know that you have no fears,
As you weather through the storm.

* * * * *

I know you will turn out all right,
But it is still my job to worry.
If they mess with you in a fight,
They will unleash a mother's fury.

Peace of War

* * * * *

In the midst of battle
The war rages on.
The bullets were flying
As the peace was withdrawn.

* * * * *

As I dove in the foxhole
To avoid the shells
I thought to myself,
"I'm in the middle of hell."

* * * * *

As I regained composure
I saw on the ground
An enemy soldier
That was hit by a round.

* * * * *

When I looked at the soldier
I saw in his face,
The fear of a child
That was lost and out of place.

* * * * *

I reached out my hand
To show I was a friend.
I tried to give him peace
For my enemy was at his end.

*****

The soldier began to speak
I didn't know what he was saying.
Although I didn't know his language
I knew that he was praying.

*****

His wound was very fatal
I knew he would not live
Then he reached out to me
As if to say, "Forgive?"

*****

Then he went with God
Or Allah if he preferred.
So I let him rest in peace
For that's what he deserved.

*****

The bombing then receded
And I had to continue on
Moving through the night,
Until the early dawn.

*****

As I tell this story
No one believes it's true,
But if two enemies can find peace
Maybe we can too.

Jon M. Nelson

Flashback

Sometimes when I hear a loud banging sound,
I'm tempted to fall and lay on the ground.
It reminds me of an enemy shooting a round,
But I look and there's no danger to be found.

* * * * *

I wake up from nightmares in the dead of night,
Because sometimes I think I'm still in the fight.
I can easily be reminded of the horrible sight,
By just a simple shadow in the moonlight.

* * * * *

The memories seem to keep haunting my mind,
And they take me back like I had hit rewind.
Hopefully someday this peace I'll be able to find,
And then I can leave the horrors behind.

* * * * *

So many things can seem to take me back,
And I always feel like I'm under attack.
Sometimes my sanity falls through the crack,
Every now and then when I have a flashback.

We Carry On

* * * * *

There are many words that will,
Forever remain unspoken.
For the loss of our loved ones,
Left us all heart-broken.

* * * * *

They defended our freedom,
And paid the ultimate price.
For the way we live our lives,
They gave their sacrifice.

* * * * *

They have given their lives,
To help us calm our fears.
But the sacrifices that they made
Will never wash away our tears.

* * * * *

The people of our nation will,
Forever be in their debt.
They are no longer with us,
For their fates had been met.

* * * * *

All that we can do now
Is to look into the past.
Cherish the times together spent,
and make those memories last.

* * * * *

Our lives may be emptier,
Now that that they may be gone.
But we must fulfill their legacy,
By the lives we carry on.

The Soldier Gives the Right

* * * * *

The soldier gives the right to bear arms,
By carrying a weapon of his own in war.
The soldier keeps us all safe from harm,
By defending us on a foreign shore.

* * * * *

The soldier gives the right to protest,
By standing up against what is wrong.
The soldier keeps us safe as we rest,
By defending through the nights so long.

* * * * *

The soldier gives the right to free speech,
By speaking out what is on his mind.
The soldier keeps our safety in reach,
By leaving his family and home behind.

* * * * *

The soldier gives the right to free press,
By the stories he will have to tell.
The soldier keeps us safe from distress,
By putting himself through a living hell.

* * * * *

The soldier gives the right to religious freedom,
By taking a moment to stop and pray.
The soldier keeps us safe from things to come,
By being on the frontline every day.

Jon M. Nelson

All in A Day's Work

* * * * *

Up in the morning before it's even light,
They work all day, then go home at night.
Giving it all through the sweat and hurt,
For them, this is all just in a day's work.

* * * * *

Training hard, they will earn their place,
With a sense of pride upon their face.
Men and women, they will work united,
Proudly they stand and never divided.

* * * * *

Defending Old Glory every single day,
They're standing for the "American way."
This is not your typical nine-to-five career,
Every day they know why they're here.

* * * * *

They do their job with honor and respect,
Because they know that they will protect.
Many hold them in the highest regard,
Because it's our nation that they guard.

* * * * *

They proudly salute the red, white, and blue,
Because it symbolizes exactly what they do.
The fate of our nation rests on their shoulders,
So be proud to depend on American soldiers.

LOVE OF A LIFETIME

Better Half

*****

I thought I had found love,
In so many times before.
Until the day I found you,
Now I could not ask for more.

*****

You are my better half,
The one who completes me.
As I look into my future,
Your love is all that I see.

*****

I feel your undying love,
Deep down within my soul.
I once was an empty shell,
But you have made me whole.

*****

I believe fate connected us,
We were meant to finally be.
My life is no longer burdened,
For your love has set me free.

*****

I always want you by my side,
My heart will beat for you.
Now I am no longer alone,
I found a love that is so true.

Everyday Valentine

* * * * *

I don't need one special day,
To show how much I love you.
I try so hard in every way,
To show my love is so true.

* * * * *

No need to give cards or flowers,
They'll eventually wither away.
Our love combined has the power,
That it will always be here to stay.

* * * * *

We don't need a candlelit dinner,
For us to be able to confess our love.
With you I am always a winner.
And for me, you are enough.

* * * * *

I don't need one day of the year,
To ask you if you will be mine.
In my heart you're always here.
You are my everyday valentine.

Jon M. Nelson

Your Love Within

* * * * *

As I gaze into your eyes,
You put me into a trance.
With your love I realize,
I've been given a chance.

* * * * *

As you hold me close,
You cast away all doubt.
Your love takes my fears and woes,
Now I cannot live without.

* * * * *

Your smile brightens my day,
I no longer have to dread.
Your love guides my way,
With the words you have said.

* * * * *

As you gently hold my hand,
I can softly feel your skin.
And as by my side you stand,
I can feel your love within.

* * * * *

As you tell me of your love,
I know the feeling is so true.
As if it was a sign from above,
Passion burns in my heart for you.

Made Me Whole

* * * * *

I could not live my life without you,
It's something I try not to think about.
I know that you are my love so true,
Of this I will never have any doubt.

* * * * *

When I wake up each new day,
I can feel your love surround me.
I try to show you in every way,
So that you will always see.

* * * * *

My heart couldn't take losing you,
I wouldn't want to go on anymore.
I feel that my life would be through,
I'd have nothing worth living for.

* * * * *

I know we share a special bond,
That cannot be ever broken.
I know that I love you beyond
Any words that are ever spoken.

* * * * *

And I know that you love me,
I can feel it deep in my soul.
With your love I feel so free,
Your love has made me whole.

Joined Hearts

* * * * *

When you hold my hand, it is my heart,
And that is where I will want to start.
If you're the one to ever feel the pain,
It is my tears that will fall like the rain.

* * * * *

Our hearts are joined together as one.
If your life should end, then mine is done.
You are all that I could ever ask for.
In this life, I will need nothing more.

* * * * *

If your heart should feel the sorrow,
Mine would not want to face tomorrow.
Your love will always be everything to me,
That is all I will ever really need to see.

* * * * *

As you feel the power of the love we need,
If you are wounded, I'm the one who'll bleed.
If the love we share were to ever be gone,
I would not have the strength to carry on.

* * * * *

I will use your love as my guiding light,
So as I may see in the darkest night.
If it is your heart I should ever break,
Then it is my life that shall have to forsake.

The Reason

* * * * *

The reason my heart still beats,
Because you hold it in your hand.
The reason that I don't fall down,
Because you always help me stand.

* * * * *

The reason that I still breathe,
Because you take my breath away.
The reason that I can still hear,
Because "I love you," that you say.

* * * * *

The reason that I can still see,
Because of your smiling face.
The reason that I still dream,
Because I'm taken to a magic place.

* * * * *

The reason that I don't get lost,
Because you are my guiding light.
The reason that my life's complete,
Because you just fit in so right.

* * * * *

The reason I haven't gone astray,
Because of your love that I found.
The reason that my world is better,
Because you are my solid ground.

Heavenly Bliss

* * * * *

Ever since you came into my life,
You have set my heart at ease.
I feel so comfortable around you,
And you're so easy to please.

* * * * *

I can always pour my heart out,
And in you I can always confide.
We can always laugh together,
And my tears you have dried.

* * * * *

I know your love without a word,
With a glance you say so much.
And when you hold me, I can feel,
How much passion is in your touch.

* * * * *

You hold my heart with a gentle hand,
And your lips have a tender kiss.
In your presence I feel such a warmth,
That puts me in a heavenly bliss.

I Love You More

* * * * *

I love you more than I could ever express,
Even with my love that I always confess.
I try to show you just how much I care,
With all the memories and moments we share.

* * * * *

I love you more than I could ever explain,
As your love takes away all of my pain.
I try to show you just exactly how I feel,
With the passion we share that is so real.

* * * * *

I love you more than I could ever define,
As your essence is so ever divine.
I try to show just exactly what I see,
When I feel your heart beat next to me.

* * * * *

I love you more than you'll ever realize,
As we stare deep into each other's eyes.
I try to tell you exactly how much I love,
But I'd never be able to tell you enough.

Then I Met You

* * * * *

I've been through hardships and through sorrow.
I never knew what to expect tomorrow.
I had given up on love and was about to give in.
Then I met you, and my new life could begin.

* * * * *

I'd been in love before and had happiness too,
But deep down I knew it wasn't really true.
I guess I didn't know what love was all about,
Then I met you, and I seemed to lose all doubt.

* * * * *

My heart had been broken and healed before,
And every time it happened, I came back for more.
I knew it could happen, but I never knew when,
Then I met you, and I know it won't happen again.

* * * * *

I've lived a full life but have had some regrets.
I've done things in my life that I'd rather forget.
Looking back now, I wonder how did it last.
Then I met you, and I didn't dwell on the past.

* * * * *

I look forward to tomorrow and what life has in store,
With you, every day is happiness, and I can't wait for more.
My life was missing pieces, and all I felt was defeat.
Then I met you, and I can say that my life is now complete.

Your Love

*****

Your love is what keeps me going,
When I feel I can't go anymore.
Your love makes it worthwhile,
When I wonder what I'm living for.

*****

Your love is so deep inside me,
When I wonder how you feel.
Your love makes my life whole,
As all the broken pieces heal.

*****

Your love is my guiding light,
When I get lost along the way.
Your love will be my sunshine,
As I start out each new day.

*****

Your love will lead the way,
As I journey down this road.
Your love is what lifts me up,
As I carry on a heavy load.

*****

Your love gives me my strength,
During moments when I feel weak.
Your love is all that I will need,
There's no more reason to seek.

You Are

* * * * *

You are my rock,
the one I'll always lean upon,
The one I want to see,
when I wake in the dawn.
You are my shoulder,
when I feel I need to cry,
The one who loves me,
without having to try.

* * * * *

You are my heaven,
when I need to say a prayer.
The one who will no matter what,
always be there.
You are my helping hand,
to grab me if I fall.
The one to help me through,
when I've hit a wall.

* * * * *

You are my angel,
to guide me along the way.
The one that I will love,
even more every day.
You are my life,
and I could not ask for more.
The one who gives me wings,
as I want to soar.

Muse

* * * * *

Not only are you the one that I desire,
You also are the one to truly inspire.
You always seem to have an insight,
And because of that, I am able to write.

* * * * *

My thoughts flow easy because of you,
And you're the reason my heart beats true.
You allow my inner thoughts to be heard,
And I am able to put them all into words.

* * * * *

Your inspiration always surrounds me,
Therefore my thoughts are running free.
My love for you is one of my inspirations,
And it is such a wonderful sensation.

* * * * *

With your eyes you can tell a story,
And our passion is bound for glory.
These ideas you give me I'm able to use,
Because you're my love and my muse.

Wedding Vow

* * * * *

Tonight as I unite with my best friend,
We'll share a love that will never end.
As we stand together as husband and wife,
It'll be happiness for the rest of our life.

* * * * *

You're more than just a dream come true,
My world is blessed now that I have you.
I'm reminded every time I see your face,
Why I fell in love with you in the first place.

* * * * *

I promise to love and treasure you always,
And be there for you the rest of my days.
With a love like ours you can't compare,
To any other love it wouldn't be fair.

* * * * *

Romeo and Juliet would even be jealous,
They could not share the love between us.
Looking at our love there can be no equal,
Nobody can duplicate or make a sequel.

* * * * *

Today as I proudly follow my heart,
For the rest of our lives, this is the start.
With you I will always go that extra mile,
As we walk together back down the aisle.

HUMAN NATURE

Through a Baby's Eyes

* * * * *

As I look out into the strange world,
I have no idea what to expect.
And as I see the dangers surround me,
I wonder who'll be there to protect.

* * * * *

I see a lot of pain and suffering,
I wonder who will bring them peace.
And as I look upon humanity,
Will this hatred ever decrease?

* * * * *

When I gaze upon the human race,
I am still too young to judge.
As I see the way they treat others,
I wonder if they'll ever budge.

* * * * *

I know my vision is still clouded,
For I haven't experienced life yet.
But when I open my eyes and see,
Humanity is our own biggest threat.

* * * * *

So I try to close my eyes to see,
And hopefully things can change.
As I try to see us loving each other,
I know the feeling will be strange.

Shed a Tear

When the emotions sometimes run wild,
The sadness consumes me like a child.
When I'm scared, I won't hide my fear,
I'm not too ashamed to shed a tear.

As the hurt puts my entire body in pain,
And the blood courses through my veins,
As I struggle to try to keep my head clear,
I'm not too ashamed to shed a tear.

Even when everything is going wrong,
I do my best to try to always stay strong.
When I don't want to look in a mirror,
I'm not too ashamed to shed a tear.

Even when all the confusion sets in,
And the entire world is covered in sin.
When everything still seems so unclear,
I'm not too ashamed to shed a tear.

After all the times people had to forsake,
And after all the times I've seen heartache,
I can now start to see things so clear,
I'm not too ashamed to shed a tear.

Jon M. Nelson

Pay It Forward

*****

When you have the chance, lend a hand.
Don't be afraid to try to take a stand.
Pay it forward, expect nothing back.
Compassion is something we all lack.

*****

A word of kindness is sometimes in need,
So is the chance to commit a good deed.
Pay it forward, take nothing in return.
Compassion is something we all can learn.

*****

If you see the need, follow your heart,
Helping others out will always be a start.
Pay it forward and pass on the charity,
Compassion is out there, we all will see.

*****

Help someone out with a life-changing event,
Let someone feel that you were heaven-sent.
Pay it forward, all the kindness inside,
Compassion is out there, it hasn't died.

*****

Show your neighbor what they're worth,
And the reason that you're on this earth.
Pay it forward without ever any regret.
Compassion is here, let us not forget.

Leave Your Mark

*****

When you're told you can't go on,
Or that you don't have what it takes.
Give it your all to prove them wrong,
And that they have made a mistake.

*****

If someone makes you feel worthless,
And fills your head up full of doubt,
Give everything and nothing less,
Show them what you're all about.

*****

We all have some kind of purpose here,
So show the world what you're worth.
Embrace your life without any fear,
While you're here upon this earth.

*****

You'll be heard if you raise your voice,
You can't start a fire without a spark.
It's your life so you must make a choice,
To always attempt to leave your mark.

Precious Smile

* * * * *

As you gaze upon their precious smile,
You'll see what makes it all worthwhile.
You can see how fragile life can really be,
As you gently hold them so delicately.

* * * * *

A precious smile is something you gaze upon,
when you really need a reason to go on.
You can see the innocence in their face,
As they continue learning about this place.

* * * * *

Their precious smile will be like a gift,
When you are down it should surely uplift.
As you deal with life and try to cope,
One look you'll know that there's hope.

* * * * *

With the precious smile you can see,
That we will all be able to be set free.
When you're confused and try to understand,
Just know that life will be in good hands.

* * * * *

As the precious smile reflects back at you,
You may wonder what exactly to do.
As the human race continues to thrive,
Now you know it'll be able to survive.

Unconditional Kindness

* * * * *

Every time you turn around,
there's always someone there.
Anytime you feel on your own,
there is someone who'll care.

* * * * *

Sometimes it just takes a smile
to brighten someone's day.
Just remember that kind words
can always go a long way.

* * * * *

Don't be afraid to lend a hand
to someone that's in need.
You'd be surprised how often
they will return the deed.

* * * * *

You will never be left alone,
if you search into your heart.
You can close the distance,
no matter how far apart.

* * * * *

Unconditional kindness
is such a precious gift.
When you follow your heart,
the feeling will uplift.

Jon M. Nelson

A Solution

* * * * *

As I look at the wreckage of the past,
I hope the future will bring a change.
I'm surprised humanity was able to last,
But our potential has unlimited range.

* * * * *

So many men have had too much pride,
It's been going on way too long.
Because of this, too many have died,
And yet we still don't see the wrong.

* * * * *

As we look upon our fellow man,
There is a place here for us all.
We all must help and do what we can,
Before we all take the final fall.

* * * * *

The wars and hatred have divided,
We all seem to have lost connection.
But our fate has not yet been decided,
We still can make a big correction.

* * * * *

Life is too fragile to survive all the hate.
If we dig down deep, we'll find a solution,
But we have not yet sealed our fate,
So there's a chance to make resolution.

Open Mind

* * * * *

The world is overrun by violence,
Which absolutely makes no sense.
People could try to be more kind,
If we would see with an open mind.

* * * * *

There are too many children crying,
And way too many soldiers dying.
There is peace we'll be able to find,
If we would see with an open mind.

* * * * *

The world has too many lost souls,
That cannot find their place or roles.
Nobody should ever be left behind,
If we face the world with an open mind.

* * * * *

So many are viewed by their tone of skin,
And never judged by their beauty within.
How could the world ever be so blind?
We must see others with an open mind.

* * * * *

Our humanity lately is becoming lost,
And what will be the ultimate cost?
Back to our roots there's a way to remind,
If we would see with an open mind.

Life's Journey

* * * * *

As we journey through our lives,
We all take separate paths.
Sometimes they're filled with sorrow,
Other times they're full of laughs.

* * * * *

There's no exact destination,
We just follow where it goes.
We travel until our journey ends,
When that is, nobody knows.

* * * * *

We all make big decisions,
As to different roads we'll take.
We all learn from accomplishments,
And mistakes that we will make.

* * * * *

What will lie ahead of us?
No one can make that call.
But we all need someone with us,
To pick us up after we fall.

* * * * *

In life our paths will cross,
We won't always be alone.
We've seen what's behind us,
But our future remains unknown.

Always Follow Your Dreams

* * * * *

Always follow your dreams,
Don't let them fade away.
If you lose sight of your goal,
It will haunt you someday.

* * * * *

Always follow your dreams,
As you shoot for the stars.
Nothing will be out of reach,
If you're willing to go far.

* * * * *

Always follow your dreams,
You just have to believe.
No one can ever stop you,
If you're willing to achieve.

* * * * *

Always follow your dreams,
No matter how silly they appear.
When others push them away,
Just pull your dreams near.

United World

* * * * *

When we stop all the fighting and the wars do cease,
Then we'll all live together with love and peace.
When labels become a thing of the past,
Then no one is first and no one is last.

* * * * *

When people stop putting each other down,
Then the walls of hatred will come crumbling down.
When it doesn't matter—the color of your skin,
Then no one will lose and everyone wins.

* * * * *

When the oceans and land are clean once again,
And we can all love our fellow man.
If we all work together, we can get it done,
The world united together as one.

Last Thing We Need

*****

Some people come into our lives,
Not knowing where they belong.
They may ask for our help because,
They just may not be strong.

*****

We may try to do all that we can,
But in the end it wasn't enough.
Our helping hands my fall short,
Because it was just too tough.

*****

Some people just may think that,
There is absolutely no way out.
They will try to end it all because,
Their life is just so full of doubt.

*****

They think the world's against them,
And that there may be no chance.
They keep falling and giving up,
They aren't willing to take a stance.

*****

We must stand strong and be willing,
To stand for them at their side.
For the last thing we need,
Is to lose someone else to suicide.

Jon M. Nelson

Heart of Gold

* * * * *

You always give of yourself,
expecting nothing in return.
The way you always care,
is something we all should learn.

* * * * *

The brighter side of life,
is something you always see.
You always see the good,
and the best of humanity.

* * * * *

Every life is precious,
in your beautiful eyes.
The good in every person,
you'll always recognize.

* * * * *

You're always more than willing,
to lend a helping hand.
Looking out for others,
is where you take a stand.

* * * * *

You set a great example,
for others to emulate.
The way you treat others,
is a beautiful character trait.

* * * * *

Don't let anyone change you,
always be this bold.
You're a diamond in the rough,
with a heart of gold.

Impression

* * * * *

Some people come into your life,
that make an impression in your heart.
They never do quite fade away,
through all the years and miles apart.

* * * * *

The feelings shared between you,
may never seem to fade away.
They leave such an impact,
that will always be there to stay.

* * * * *

It's hard to let someone go,
when deep down you still care.
Especially when there may be,
So many memories that you share.

* * * * *

The times you spent together,
made a part of who you are.
And they remain a part of you,
no matter how close or far.

* * * * *

Many times in your life, you make,
a choice of who you know.
And very often in your life,
you choose not to let them go.

A Mother's Love

* * * * *

From the human race to animals in the wild,
There's a special bond between a mother and child.
Right up until the very last breath in her lungs,
She'll do what she must to protect her young.

* * * * *

A mother will always go above and beyond,
To always ensure that unbreakable bond.
And every time that push comes to shove,
There is just no match for a mother's love.

* * * * *

Whenever they're involved in such a strife,
A mother will protect with her own life.
A mother will always find a way to disarm,
All the dangers to keep them from harm.

* * * * *

The bond between them is impossible to break,
And the love between them you can't forsake.
A mother will show her children respect,
And she will die trying to always protect.

Father

* * * * *

As he looks down at his precious child's face,
He's always there to offer that protective embrace.
He'll do what he can to ensure they're raised right,
And always stand as a beacon or a guiding light.

* * * * *

He'll protect them from harm any way he's able,
And do what he can to put food on their table.
There are many things he will be able to teach,
And if he needs to, there'll be a time to preach.

* * * * *

He'll always be there to dry away their tears,
And do what he can to help them face their fears.
As he watches them grow, there's a sense of pride,
And he hopes that in him, they can always confide.

* * * * *

He'll always listen to their hopes and dreams,
No matter how silly or impossible they may seem.
He'll always show them the ultimate respect,
And he'll do what he must to always protect.

Stepdad

* * * * *

Now that your mother has become my wife,
You will always be a big part of my life.
I know I could never take your dad's place,
But in your heart I hope you have a space.

* * * * *

I'll love you as if you were my own child,
Even the times you feel like running wild.
Our time together has given us a start,
And now you have a place in my heart.

* * * * *

With you and your mother we're a family,
And the love we share should be easy to see.
Don't think I'm taking your mother away,
Because you will be with us every day.

* * * * *

And as I raise you like I would my own,
Know that you'll never have to be alone.
I'll be there to support you any way I can,
Today as a family our new life has began.

Human Race

*****

Everywhere you look you will see,
The downfall of our humanity.
So much crime and lack of respect,
We'll never know what to expect.

*****

Try as you may, it's hard to tell,
Why humanity is under this spell.
If people are willing to take a stance,
Than mankind can still have a chance.

*****

There is still goodness out there,
But many are just unsure where.
If you look deep down, it's inside,
You just can't let it continue to hide.

*****

For too long, humanity has destroyed,
And every generation it leaves a void.
Yet our future is still so uncertain,
But it's not over till we close the curtain.

*****

Humanity may be its own biggest threat,
But the human race is not gone yet.
There are those who will never give in,
And be so influenced by all of this sin.

* * * * *

If you search and follow your heart,
There's a chance we can make a new start.
The world can be a better place,
If we can all unite as one human race.

Teach the Children

* * * * *

Hate and prejudice are traits that are learned,
And because of that, so many people get burned.
They live their lives by the way they're taught,
Never realizing all the hatred they have brought.

* * * * *

They think they are superior and should dominate.
With mind-sets such as this, what will be our fate?
When we are young, people make an impression,
So "What will we be teaching them?" is the question.

* * * * *

Children watch and learn from our actions and words,
Our future depends on what they've seen and heard.
We must be able to teach them right from wrong,
And how easy it should be for us to get along.

* * * * *

We need to teach the children the right way to live,
To love your fellow man and be willing to give.
If the future generations do not repeat the past,
We all can have hope that humanity will last.

Earned

The sun will rise, and it will set,
The world will always turn.
Mistakes will often be made,
They are lessons we will learn.

Don't ever give up so easily,
There's something you'll yearn.
When you dig down deep inside,
There's a passion that will burn.

There will be many obstacles,
Around just about every turn.
The more effort that you put in,
It will be something really earned.

Learn to Crawl

* * * * *

When it seems that all you do,
Is to stumble and fall,
Remember before you walk, you
Have to learn to crawl.

* * * * *

There are many obstacles to
Climb before you reach the top.
Even though they may hold you
Back, it's no reason to stop.

* * * * *

Always look forward and keep
Moving toward you goal.
Sometimes you have to search deep
Down into your soul.

Climbing

* * * * *

I have been down to the lowest level,
Where I stood face-to-face with the devil.
But I had to raise myself up higher,
And was able to get up out of the fire.

* * * * *

I had dug myself into a deep, dark hole,
Where the emptiness would fill my soul.
I had found a way to raise my spirit,
To be able to get up out of that pit.

* * * * *

I have been to the bottom of the abyss,
Where I found that the world was amiss.
I had to climb up toward the light,
And I was able to escape that fight.

* * * * *

I've stood at the base of the mountain,
Where I knew I'd have to climb again.
But I would never be willing to stop,
If I ever wanted to reach the top.

* * * * *

I have now reached the highest point,
And up here I hope I don't disappoint.
There's only one place left for me to go,
As I can see the stars beginning to show.

Always Be

*****

There will always be satisfaction,
If we can always be in the action.
There will always be a reaction,
If there'll always be an attraction.

*****

We'll always be in the participation,
Since there will always be creation.
And there will always be anticipation,
Since there will always be devastation.

*****

Now our minds will always be learning,
And the passion will always be burning.
Of course we will always be earning,
For something we'll always be yearning.

*****

Our minds will always be knowing,
As our lives are always growing.
And the humanity will always be showing,
As our debts we'll always be owing.

*****

Our lives will always be making corrections,
Because we'll always be choosing directions.
We'll always be put into different sections,
Because we'll always be waiting for final inspections.

Break of Dawn

* * * * *

Celebrate your life in every way,
Make the most out of each day.
Another part of your life is gone,
When you face the break of dawn.

* * * * *

Always live your life to the fullest,
And always strive to do your best.
There's no guarantee life goes on,
Until you face the break of dawn.

* * * * *

Let your feelings for loved ones show,
Every day you should let them know.
Because tomorrow you may be gone,
There may not be a break of dawn.

* * * * *

Make an impact before you leave,
Give others a reason to always believe.
Let the picture of your life be drawn,
On the canvas of the break of dawn.

* * * * *

Live each moment with a sense of pride,
And let the world know you tried.
Always make sure your legacy lives on,
Even long after your last break of dawn.

Don't Cry for Me

* * * * *

I hope that when I leave here,
It won't be without a trace.
Hopefully at some point in life,
I put a smile upon your face.
I tried to stop the hatred,
And the evil help erase.
I did what I could to make,
This world a better place.

* * * * *

I tried to make a difference,
And unite the world as one.
But now it's up to others,
To help the task get done.
I want you to remember,
All the good times and fun.
Remember my life as beauty,
Like the setting of the sun.

* * * * *

Don't shed any tears for me,
I'd like for you to celebrate.
Not because I'm no longer here,
But for what I tried to create.
There can possibly be a world,
Without prejudice and hate.
It is in the human nature,
I guess you could call it fate.

* * * * *

Even though my curtain closed,
The show must still go on.
For each day will continue,
With the start of each new dawn.
I ask that my legacy will be
attempted to continue on.
Celebrate what I did for you,
Don't cry for me after I'm gone.

Continuous Motion

* * * * *

As I search the horizon for a new beginning,
I always wonder what tomorrow will bring.
As the sun rises, it triggers a new day,
But now will I get lost along the way?

* * * * *

Yesterday was when I left it all behind.
Today I search to see exactly what I'll find.
The present is now so I've no need to wait.
I can't put it off and try to hesitate.

* * * * *

The future is unseen, not knowing what's ahead.
Yesterday is the past, and it's been left for dead.
Time is a continuous motion that cannot halt.
If I don't make the best of it, it's my own fault.

Birthday Child

* * * * *

As you get older and begin to mature,
You'll find times of which you're unsure.
This is natural, a process as you grow,
And there are things you still won't know.

* * * * *

As you grow older, things will be strange,
And you'll notice many things to change.
Someday soon you know the day will come,
Before you're able to enjoy your freedom.

* * * * *

Remember someone's watching over you,
So that your future will be bright and true.
Be sure to always listen to the inner voices,
So that you'll always make the right choices.

* * * * *

So as you celebrate this day of your birth,
Know there's a reason you're on this earth.
You bring joy and happiness to those around,
Be sure to lay your foundation on solid ground.

Lullaby

* * * * *

As you get settled down on your bed,
Be sure that you rest your weary head.
You can drift off as you close your eyes,
For I'm going to sing you a lullaby.

* * * * *

It's time to settle down for the night,
And just relax as I turn off the light.
There is no reason to fear or cry,
Because I'm going to sing you a lullaby.

* * * * *

Rest your body and drift off to sleep,
May your dreams be peaceful and deep.
You can get the rest in which you rely,
As I begin to sing you this lullaby.

* * * * *

Forget about all of your pain and woes,
As you snuggle up from head to toes.
Tomorrow is another day you can try,
After I sing you to sleep with a lullaby.

A Friend Will

*****

A friend will help lift you up,
When you're knocked to the ground.
A friend will stand by your side,
When no one else is around.

*****

A friend will share their secrets,
And will always protect yours.
A friend will help you through
All the blocked and locked doors.

*****

A friend will never judge you,
When everyone else looks down.
A friend will try to save you,
When you feel like you may drown.

*****

A friend will always be there,
Just when you least expect.
A friend will not turn away,
They'll give you the respect.

*****

A friend will always listen,
If you just need to scream.
A friend will never laugh,
At your fantasies and dreams.

* * * * *

A friend will stand beside you,
As you stand to face your fears.
A friend will hold out their hand,
To help you dry away your tears.

Take and Give

* * * * *

If I feel that I have hit rock bottom,
I will find a way back to the top.
When it feels like I can't keep going,
That's when I know that I can't stop.

* * * * *

If I have to pick the easy wrong
Or choose the difficult right,
I know that I will be at peace,
Because I'll always win that fight.

* * * * *

When I'm crawling through the dirt,
I know that I will come out clean.
Because even though it is hidden,
I will make my strength be seen.

* * * * *

When I get pushed to the edge,
I will find a way back to the center.
If my fantasies and dreams all exit,
There will be new ones that will enter.

* * * * *

If all my hopes vanish into thin air,
I will still stand on solid ground.
When it seems that all is lost,
All my hopes can still be found.

* * * * *

If I ever get lost in the darkness,
I will always look for the light.
For if I ever become blinded,
I'll find a way to have the sight.

* * * * *

No matter what, I will move forward,
Even when the world holds me back.
I always try to keep the future bright,
For it will eventually fade to black.

* * * * *

I look at life and try not to condemn,
I find it easier to always forgive.
In this world there is too much take,
But there are still those willing to give.

Color Blind

* * * * *

We all come from different backgrounds,
No two people are the same.
If you take a good look around,
You'll wonder what is really in a name.

* * * * *

When I look upon this world,
There are so many unpleasant sights.
So many things have unfurled,
That we've almost lost our human rights.

* * * * *

Our humanity has almost been lost,
You can see it in a child's face.
Human life is the ultimate cost.
What's to become of the human race?

* * * * *

As I look out I see the love is gone,
So many judge by the tone of skin.
We all must go and look beyond,
Search for the beauty and heart within.

* * * * *

We are all in this world together,
We must stand and reunite.
Learn to love your fellow brother,
For what we'll do is right.

Jon M. Nelson

* * * * *

If we put our differences aside,
And look together, we will find,
That if we all stand side by side,
We all can become color blind.

Children Have Tomorrow

* * * * *

We must pass on our happiness and our sorrows,
To our children, for they own tomorrow.
The world is now theirs to take care,
We did our best, but now we must share.

* * * * *

The children hold the key to the truth.
The world is now theirs, for they have youth.
The world we had was just to borrow,
We must save what we have to pass on tomorrow.

* * * * *

The children hold the future in the palms of their hands.
They must work together and united they'll stand
We must lead the children in the right direction,
By showing love and lots of affection.

* * * * *

The world belongs to the children we leave.
The future looks brighter, we all must believe.

Road Less Traveled

* * * * *

Sometimes the road less traveled,
doesn't have to be that way.
People may sometimes be too scared,
to try something new each day.

* * * * *

Try going off the beaten path,
every once in a great while.
Even though it may take longer,
and you'll go that extra mile.

* * * * *

Try stopping to smell the roses,
or exploring something new.
You'll never know what you find,
along the journey you may ensue.

Begin the Hunt

* * * * *

You cannot find the rainbow,
Without waiting out the storm.
If you suffer the blizzard,
You'll appreciate the warm.

* * * * *

When you don't do your best,
You may feel at your worst.
If you start to feel the heat,
You'll need to fulfill your thirst.

* * * * *

You may be in the darkness,
In order to find the light.
And everything may go wrong,
Before something goes right.

* * * * *

Life can sometimes turn its back,
But you must put up a strong front.
Sometimes you may feel like prey,
Before you can begin the hunt.

Direction

* * * * *

I've burned too many bridges,
To go back across the river.
I could try to swim back across,
But the coldness made me shiver.

* * * * *

I've stepped off the straight and narrow,
So many times that I have lost track.
Since then, I had lost my way,
I wondered if I could ever get back.

* * * * *

My moral compass was broken,
It would lead me the wrong way.
I had no conscience to guide me,
So I would always be led astray.

* * * * *

I've broken so many hearts,
And been left picking up the pieces.
When I tried to make things right,
I kept falling through the creases.

* * * * *

But then I found a guiding light,
That brightened up my path.
I could see the error of my ways,
And what was left in the aftermath.

* * * * *

Whenever I feel misguided,
I can make that big correction.
Now I've turned my life around,
I'm heading in the right direction.

A Child Is

* * * * *

A child is precious and should be treated as such,
They should be held and caressed with a gentle touch.
A child is the future and should be shown the way,
They should be taught by the things we do and say.

* * * * *

A child is your life and should be the biggest part,
They should always be loved with all of your heart.
A child is a miracle sent down from heaven above,
They should always be given unconditional love.

* * * * *

A child is a blessing, and there is no reason to doubt,
They should be something you cannot live without.
A child is your strength to help you through it all,
They should be the reason that you don't want to fall.

Common Ground

* * * * *

Where exactly did our priorities go?
This is something we may never know.
Family values are a thing of the past,
And our connections don't seem to last.

* * * * *

The wars are senseless and have no point,
And the evening news will always disappoint.
There are children starving across the earth,
They are treated like they have no worth.

* * * * *

Most big cities now are overrun by thugs,
And too many people are high on drugs.
In this world there's too much violence,
Because too many people lack the sense.

* * * * *

Too many women and children get abused,
Which is a state that leaves us all confused.
We all must be able learn to rise above,
And be willing to help spread the love.

* * * * *

What can we do to turn this world around?
We all must find some type of common ground.
We're all in this together on this planet,
But yet we are our own biggest threat.

Jon M. Nelson

Reflections

* * * * *

Life can be a gamble,
but you still must roll the dice.
Even if you are a winner,
there still will be a sacrifice.

* * * * *

For every step forward,
there still will be a setback.
You must pull the reins tight,
for life will cut you no slack.

* * * * *

As you gaze into a mirror,
be very proud of the reflection.
When you feel at your worst,
Remember that there's no perfection.

* * * * *

Before you can take flight,
you must stand on solid ground.
Before your innocence is lost,
your purpose must be found.

* * * * *

You must break your silence,
if your opinion is to be voiced.
Sometimes you break tradition,
in order to make the right choice.

* * * * *

Stay on the straight and narrow,
but the truth can sometimes bend.
As your new adventure begins,
it must also come to an end.

How Long Will We Last?

* * * * *

I've seen many things, and I still believe,
You have to give if you want to receive.
Do unto others as they would do to you,
It's harder to find for this to be true.

* * * * *

Random acts of kindness you seldom see,
Just thinking of ourselves, how will we be free?
There's a time and a purpose for everything.
And we all wait for that time when we can sing.

* * * * *

I believe that the world belongs to us all,
So why do so many people have to fall?
It seems like no one is willing to share,
And it breaks down because none of them care.

* * * * *

The world is big enough for us all to live,
But nobody seems to be willing to give.
As we look to the future, how long will we last,
If we keep making the same mistakes of the past?

Live Each Moment

* * * * *

Live each moment as if it's your last,
Relive those memories from your past.
Nothing in this life can be certain,
At anytime they can draw the curtain.

* * * * *

There's no guarantee you'll have tomorrow,
There's never any more time you can borrow.
You'll never understand the circumstance,
In this life you will only get one chance.

* * * * *

You must live your life for all it's worth,
And leave your mark upon this earth.
What you leave behind is your legacy,
But it's up to you what that will be.

* * * * *

Show the ones you love that you care,
You may not get another chance to share.
Always cherish those precious moments,
Because each one could be heaven-sent.

* * * * *

Make your voice be heard while you're around,
It will be silenced when you're in the ground.
We take this life for granted way too often,
But at anytime we could be put into a coffin.

We're All in This Together

We're all in this together, so let's enjoy the ride.
Sometimes we just have to swallow our pride.
Are we really different since we don't look the same?
We are all human beings, this isn't just a game.

We're all in this together here upon this earth,
And everyone deep down has some kind of worth.
We have no room for prejudice, so why must we hate?
We must learn to get along before it is too late.

We're all in this together; we only get one chance.
We should all enjoy the music during life's dance.
There is no reason why we can't follow our heart,
If you love your fellow man, that will be a start.

We're all in this together, everyone can agree,
Until we stop the hatred, we'll never be truly free.
Life is too short to be angry all of the time,
All this hatred and war are nothing but a crime.

Four-Letter Word

* * * * *

Because of this word, so many are abused,
And also why people always feel used.
It is the reason there is so much crime,
It's been around since the beginning of time.

* * * * *

It is a word that so many people despise,
And the reason there are so many lies.
It is often the cause of too many wars,
And why opportunity closes the doors.

* * * * *

Prejudices will often be the root cause,
Because many people look for the flaws.
It is the reason there's so much violence,
And why so many things don't make sense.

* * * * *

We can teach our children not to have it,
But for most adults, now it is a habit.
Peace and love are still always around,
But their echo isn't as great of a sound.

* * * * *

Because of this word, too many have died,
And rivers of tears have also been cried,
One of the ugliest obscenities ever heard,
That's why HATE is a four-letter word.

Hate Crimes

* * * * *

When violence is committed against another soul,
The aftermath is always going to take its toll.
Most people too often will turn their backs,
And do nothing to try to stop these attacks.

* * * * *

A person's religion or color is often the cause,
Because they won't take a moment to pause.
The attackers never think of the consequence,
And as a result, there is always too much violence.

* * * * *

As the human race, we're just trying to survive,
Yet every day is a struggle to just stay alive.
For no reason at all there is too much killing,
And the thought of all of this is too chilling.

* * * * *

Why should it matter what color is your skin,
Or what type of church that you worship in?
There's no reason to cause harm to another being,
Because hatred is blinding and they aren't seeing.

* * * * *

But someone being different isn't always the cause,
Some will attack others even without any flaws.
Some people are just violent because of the thrill,
And they don't care if they will maim or kill.

* * * * *

They'd rather cause harm than offer a helping hand,
Because too many people don't want to understand.
People hurting people, it happens all the time,
Wouldn't all violence be considered a hate crime?

A DARKER SIDE

Losing Game

* * * * *

Why should I even bother to try?
All I do is make the world cry.
I always attempt to give my all,
But in the end I will always fall

* * * * *

My love for the world, I do not hide,
But why do I bottle my feelings inside?
I cannot express or explain my thoughts,
So in the end it is all for naught.

* * * * *

If I don't sit and really count the cost,
How will I know what I've really lost?
In the end, we all finish the same,
Nobody can win when it's a losing game.

Bullying

* * * * *

They seem to think they're better than everyone,
And they torment other people just for fun.
Maybe it's because of their own low self-esteem,
And for some reason think that this will redeem.

* * * * *

Others are hurt by their actions and their words,
And the children's cries will often go unheard.
They do it without remorse or consequence,
But the whole idea just doesn't make sense.

* * * * *

Some children many times will live in fear,
And too often go home and shed many tears.
Others are afraid to be willing to take a stand,
And feel that nobody else will ever understand.

* * * * *

Some people watch and will do nothing to cease,
So nobody can bring the tormented child peace.
Deep down they know that bullying isn't right,
So it should be time that they stand up to unite.

Internal Choice

* * * * *

As I search deep down into my soul,
I wonder if I can make it on my own.
I wonder where in life I have a role,
I need to know if I should be all alone.

* * * * *

Will I ever need somebody by my side?
Must I always have someone there?
With whom my deepest thoughts shall I confide?
My life, with someone else, must I always share?

* * * * *

As I look back upon my life and deeply reflect,
I wonder to myself, just where did I go wrong?
Not knowing what in the future I should expect,
Shall I remain alone, or with someone should I belong?

* * * * *

Why does it feel that I always have to rush?
Exactly what am I always afraid to lose?
How come it always seems like I need to push?
Why does it always seem so difficult to choose?

* * * * *

My ego, I seem to always have to rise above.
I should always listen to my deep inner voice.
When it comes down to it and push comes to shove,
Now stand I must, and here make this internal choice.

Sorrow

* * * * *

As I feel the agony fill my veins,
It's impossible to ignore the pains.
The wretched fear fills my soul,
As my body is no longer whole.

* * * * *

The tears well up inside my eyes,
As I can't help break down and cry.
The happiness has left my heart,
While my world is falling apart.

* * * * *

I have to suffer as the light fades,
And the pain hits me like one thousand blades.
The broken heart leaves a scar,
And now I know I won't get far.

* * * * *

A fatal blow has been struck,
For now I have run out of luck.
I lay me down until tomorrow,
Only to hope there is no sorrow.

Jon M. Nelson

Crimson Rain

* * * * *

As I look all around, everything is soaked,
From all the violence that's been provoked.
Crimson rivers now flow through the street,
And it is everywhere I try to place my feet.

* * * * *

What is the purpose and sense of all this chaos,
Which causes nothing but heartache and loss?
It looks as if it had fallen from a crimson sky,
And was the cause for so many people to die.

* * * * *

After time all the innocence is washed away,
But for all this evil what price will they pay?
The color of crimson now burns my eyes,
And it hurts my ears just to hear their cries.

* * * * *

As the crimson rain keeps pouring down,
The flooding won't stop and I may drown.
It seems that this insanity will never cease,
But the tears I cry will not bring the peace.

* * * * *

I look down and cry at this dreadful sight,
For all of this suffering just isn't right.
I can sense the torture and feel the pain.
Who's responsible for this crimson rain?

Nightmare

* * * * *

The darkness soon consumes the overwhelming sky,
I move slowly through the shadows along the ground.
The overwhelming sadness soon causes me to cry,
For I cannot bear the intensity of the midnight sound.

* * * * *

A lifetime of pain is suffered in just one lonely night.
My heart sinks as I feel the looming sorrow and chaos.
The darkness does not seem to hinder my sight,
I make my way through although I feel the loss.

* * * * *

I can feel the nightmares spinning around in my head,
There is so much suffering and I can feel the pain.
As this dark evil surrounds me it is making me dread,
The distance that I've traveled with nothing to gain.

* * * * *

The evil tries to penetrate, but it will not succeed,
For the goodness somehow will manage to prevail.
Even though the wounds are painful and they bleed,
Deep down inside my heart I know I cannot fail.

* * * * *

Reality is distorted, and nothing is as it seems,
I take a closer look and realize that it's all fake.
What was the cause of these nightmarish dreams?
I will no longer wonder as I slowly begin to wake.

Insanity

* * * * *

As I sit here in the world of shattered dreams,
I realize nothing is really as it seems.
The lunacy adheres to everything around,
And chaos looms as I hear the sound.

* * * * *

No matter what I do, I can't escape the voices.
Whether right or wrong they make my choices.
I seem to be losing at the living game,
But do I really have only myself to blame?

* * * * *

As the madness begins to settle into my mind,
I wonder if there's a cure they'll be able to find.
What in my life drove me to go this insane?
I know something isn't right inside my brain.

Haunting

*****

As I hear the dark and somber tones,
Echo throughout the land,
It sends a chill down to my bones,
Knowing that I need to make a stand.

*****

The darkness consumes the atmosphere,
The hate is all around me.
I know that I must remove this fear,
In order to be set free.

*****

There is an unnerving force surrounding me,
It is a presence I can't deny.
I cannot outrun it or try to flee,
Or surely I may die.

*****

I can't see what lies in the darkness there,
There is something holding me back.
It's like an internal nightmare,
As I'm waiting for the attack.

*****

Suddenly a light breaks through the darkness,
Everything seems to be at peace.
It's all in my head, I must confess.
Now my body can be at ease.

Grave Dancer

* * * * *

As the shadows move slowly across the land,
The darkness falls and takes me by the hand.
The sounds of the nighttime begin to appear,
The eerie sounds bring out the inner fear.

* * * * *

I take a breath and hear the sounds so smooth,
For the music of darkness helps my heart sooth.
The calmness falls over me, and I get the notion,
And my body is energetically put into motion.

* * * * *

My feet start moving as I dance on the grave,
Moving in rhythm just like a Cherokee Brave.
When the dead surround me, I feel more alive,
This is the only way I can really be revived.

* * * * *

It is more than what you would ever expect,
This is the only way I know how to show respect.
As the ground glows from the moon at night,
It becomes the main source as my spotlight.

* * * * *

As I bid farewell to the newly deceased,
When I leave here, they will rest in peace.
The Grave Dancer has left his mark in this space,
Forever lasting in this eternal resting place.

Lost

* * * * *

It's nearly impossible to face reality,
As you cross the bridge to insanity.
When you head out into the unknown,
It's a journey that you must take alone.

* * * * *

As the judgment brings down the gavel,
There is a road that you'll have to travel.
When it feels everything you *do* is wrong,
You'll then realize that you don't belong.

* * * * *

In this trial there are decisions to make,
And one bad choice can be a mistake.
During this adventure it's easy to confuse,
For you never know if you'll win or lose.

* * * * *

And as curiosity gets the best of you,
You just may not always make it through.
So as you really count up all of the cost,
Decide if it was really worth it to get lost.

Isolation

* * * * *

Human contact, I must do without,
They cannot hear although I shout.
Darkness surrounds me, I can't see,
I wonder why this is happening to me.

* * * * *

I did nothing wrong, I broke no law,
I wonder if it's because of what I saw.
The echo of my voice is the only sound,
For now I know nobody else is around.

* * * * *

Life is too short, and I don't understand,
How this inner voice obeys my command.
The loneliness creates a temptation,
That still pulls me into this isolation.

GOD'S BEAUTY

We'll All Be Judged

* * * * *

If you take a look around at everyone's face,
You'll see that we're all part of the human race.
What will end up as the overall consequence,
If we continue with this senseless violence?
If all you do is look down at your fellow man,
Then you just interfere with the ultimate plan.
Yet if you are still too stubborn to budge,
Remember in the end that we'll all be judged.

* * * * *

If you simply pass by the homeless on the street,
That is out there begging for something to eat,
Remember they aren't there by their own choice.
They have lost all reason to ever again rejoice.
You can either give of your heart in some way,
Or you can totally ignore them as you turn away.
But if you aren't willing to give them a nudge,
Remember in the end that we'll all be judged.

* * * * *

Even if you may have been hurt in the past,
And have deep scars that will always last.
Others may have caused you tremendous pain,
For they may have felt they had something to gain.
You've always been told to live and let live,
You must find it down in your heart to forgive.
There is no reason to ever hold a grudge,
Remember in the end that we'll all be judged.

Thunderstorm

* * * * *

As night turns into morning,
the light is still so dim.
I listen to the warning,
as the new dawn begins.

* * * * *

I feel the ground shudder,
as the thunder shakes the skies.
My heart begins to flutter
for I can't believe my eyes.

* * * * *

As the lightning crashes,
it ripples through the air.
As I watch the flashes,
it's so hard not to stare.

* * * * *

The thunder begins to clatter,
as it screams its voice.
The sound can only shatter,
with that deafening noise.

* * * * *

The clouds begin to darken,
as the rain pours down.
The thunder is still barking,
with that somber sound.

Jon M. Nelson

* * * * *

And so before too long,
everything will be soaked.
As the storm still sings its song,
My vision becomes cloaked.

* * * * *

As the storm starts to unwind
I still can feel its power.
It's amazing what you'll find,
after the immense shower.

* * * * *

As the clouds begin to break,
and the sunlight's coming through,
I see devastation in the wake,
now that the storm is through.

* * * * *

Piercing through the clouds
the sunlight begins to shine.
As the wind removes the shrouds
it's all part of the great design.

* * * * *

A rainbow remains to signify,
that the storm is at its end,
shining brightly in the sky,
as a reminder of a Godsend.

Through It All

*****

If you feel you've hit rock bottom,
And there's no place left to fall,
When the world is out to get you,
And your back's against the wall.

*****

When it seems whenever you cry out,
Nobody will hear your call,
When life's momentum goes nowhere,
And it all has seemed to stall.

*****

If life just seems overwhelming,
And you just want to bawl,
When everything is pushing you down,
And all you can do is crawl.

*****

When everything's stacked against you,
And you're ready for a brawl,
There's always someone with you,
To help you through it all.

Jon M. Nelson

Sunset

* * * * *

The multiple colors blend in as one,
As they mask the disappearing sun.
Slowly I watch as it drifts away,
It's marking the end of another day.

* * * * *

While it fades it leaves a heavy glow,
As it performs a spectacular show.
The colors seem to paint the skies,
As I gaze at the wonder before my eyes.

* * * * *

The painted canvas looks so bright,
As it leaves behind the amazing sight.
Below the horizon it begins to fade,
With the spectacular drama it has made.

Shadow Boxer

* * * * *

As the darkness slowly begins to settle in,
I can feel the evil, the hatred, and the sin.
I'll attempt to counterbalance the fight,
When I use love, purity, and the light.

* * * * *

As the shadows around me get stronger,
I don't know if I can hold on much longer.
The demons bring an overwhelming fear,
I will state my position loud and clear.

* * * * *

The evil always tries to possess my soul,
But I feel that I have a stronger goal.
They'll always try to get the best of me,
But I will not be conquered that easily.

* * * * *

In the corner of the shadows, evil stands,
But I too will have a few helping hands.
It seems the evil around me has grown,
But I will not be fighting it on my own.

* * * * *

There's a vicious attack from the shadows,
I have a strong defense for the blows.
I stand and block and do not fight back,
For this is not my moment to attack.

* * * * *

As they try to move in to go for the kill,
The peace surrounds me as I stand still.
With a knockout blow they stood no chance,
And over this evil I do a victory dance.

I Am Not Afraid

*****

As I travel through this life every passing day,
I am not afraid of whatever comes my way.
As I continue on I see the hatred and the fears,
I am not afraid, for I am able to shed my tears.

*****

I will overcome anything that comes along,
I am not afraid, for I know my will is strong.
I look around at all the senseless violence,
I am not afraid, for in my heart lies patience.

*****

I look around at the souls unable to roam,
I am not afraid, for I know I'm going home.
Looking out I see all the hatred that they send,
I am not afraid, for I know we'll be judged in the end.

Jon M. Nelson

Man Without Sin

* * * * *

As the angels sing with heavenly grace,
The light of God shines upon his face.
A man without sin, a man without wrong,
He walks among us as he should belong.
Roaming the earth, preaching the word,
Looking upon him, you'll know he's Lord.
As he burdens the weight of the cross and our sin,
He promises us that he'll rise again.
After he arose and the heavens did burn,
He promised again that he would return.

The Snowman

* * * * *

Starting out as a handful
It gains mass as it rolls
Individually they are barely noticed
Together they cover the ground
Each as unique as a fingerprint
They share a common goal
Each one joining to the next
As the white sphere rolls around
As it rolls, it leaves a path
Of emptiness in its wake
With each passing roll and turn
The sphere increases in mass
Each one sticks together
Combining to make the sphere
As the flakes combine and roll away
It leaves nothing but the grass
When the desired size is reached
And the location set in
They begin another journey
Forming mass as they roll
Another sphere is being created
To join its counterpart
Again another path of emptiness

Jon M. Nelson

Joins the other one on the ground
The second sphere has joined the first
To create a larger mass
But the flakes are not finished yet
There's still work to do
Another sphere begins its journey
To complete this work of art
At last the final sphere has joined
But the creation is not through
Now some flakes are sacrificed
To help create the shape
The mass is being sculpted
To obtain its final form
Some objects are added to complete
This wonder which they created
Now here they stay…United.
until the earth is warm

Path of God

As I follow in his footsteps, I know he'll lead the way.
I get closer to heaven with every passing day.
I'm on the path of righteousness, leading toward the Lord.
Praying and listening as he speaks his mighty word.
With every passing step, I'm reaching closer to my goal.
The saving and cleansing of my once tortured soul,
Whenever I have doubts, whenever I have fear,
I always reach my heart toward God, for I know that he is near.
Searching for the truth, I know I will not be deceived,
I'm following the path of God, this I do believe.

Jon M. Nelson

Forces Stand against Me

* * * * *

Forces stand against me,
But I still will not stop.
I'll find a way around,
To make it to the top.

* * * * *

Forces stand against me,
But they won't hold me back.
I need to have focus,
For they'll cut me no slack.

* * * * *

Forces stand against me,
But I say, "Bring it on."
I don't want it easy,
Or the challenge is gone.

Prince of Peace

* * * * *

He was born under the brightest star,
And three wise men had traveled so far.
They came bearing gifts for the baby,
Placed in a manger for them to see.

* * * * *

The angels smiled and began to sing,
Over the birth of the King of kings.
The savior had arrived on to the earth,
And they all were aware of his worth.

* * * * *

The child needed to be protected,
For his birth had been predicted.
He would be the one for our salvation,
And the ruler over a powerful nation.

* * * * *

He would perform miracles so they'd believe,
And bring happiness when they would grieve.
They all knew that he was the one,
As they looked upon him, the holy Son.

* * * * *

He was later betrayed by one of his own,
But he knew that he wouldn't die alone.
He asked his father to forgive them,
And also that he would not condemn.

* * * * *

The Prince of Peace until his last breath,
And continued to be even after his death.
He arose from the dead to return again;
We're just waiting for the moment when.